This Land of Legend
Arkansas Poems by Ruth Couch

Illustrations by Jerry Poole and Foy Lisenby

R☙SE
PUBLISHING
COMPANY, INC.

Little Rock, Arkansas
1992

Couch, Ruth.
This land of legend.
Illustrations by Jerry Poole and Foy Lisenby

Bibliography: p.
1.   American poetry -- 20th century -- Arkansas.   I.
Title
PS3553.073T4 1990   811.54 Cou   LC card number 90-062573
ISBN 0-914546-88-0

Book design by Elizabeth F. Shores

Cover design by David Greene

Dedication

The author and the artists present this book in loving memory of our friends and mentors, Dr. George and Mrs. Margie Harrod. The Harrods taught at DeQueen High School, where Dr. Harrod was an art instructor who inspired the young Jerry Poole to develop his own talents.

Later, Dr. and Mrs. Harrod taught and were administrators at Southern State College, now Southern Arkansas University at Magnolia. While there, they were instructors and role models for Ruth Couch. The Harrods taught us to love stories, treasure our state, and enjoy sharing our stories and illustrations with others. We hope they would be pleased with our efforts.

Contents

PREFACE   vii

THE POEMS

The Indians at Evergreen   1
Spirit Lake   2
The Butter Fight   4
Petit Jean   6
The Legend of War Eagle   9
War Eagle -- The Meeting   12
White Oak Silver Mine   14
The Lazy Man   16
The Cat-Bag Legend   19
The Crossett Light   20
The Crossett Light Revisited   22
The Ha'nt Tree   24
The Smallden Well   26
Belle Starr's Race   28
A Highway Shrine   30
Robin Hood of Civil War Arkansas   33
Hardin's Inn   35
The Spirit Dog   37
The Land Avenges   40
The Last Ride Home   43
The Late-Night Shortcut   45
Aunt Mollie's Warning   48
The Prisoner from Little Rock   51
The Hook   53
The Valley of Vapors   55
The Shopping-Mall Specter   57
The Hitchhiker of 1980   58
The Black Lady Walks at Henderson State   60
Carry A. Nation   63
The Roosters Crow for Christmas   66

BIBLIOGRAPHY   69

Preface

The poems in this book are based on stories that I have read or heard. Some of the stories are factual; some are traditional, and some, perhaps, are even fabrications. Many of the poems deal with the supernatural. Some present historical or pseudo-historical information.

The poems are told in a simple style resembling some ballads. They are straightforward narratives; little attempt is made to call up emotion. The stories themselves should provide all the feeling necessary. The poems rhyme, some being written in four-line stanzas, some in couplets. The language is simple, but the characters and the stories are treated respectfully, not in a sneering fashion. The rhythm is fairly regular, so that some of the poems perhaps could be sung. The story line is followed rather sparsely; not many details are used.

Although some of the stories are traditional, it should be noted that not all of them represent old material. The desire for a story, even one with supernatural elements, is by no means a characteristic of long-past times. Not all of the stories have rural settings; several urban legends are represented. The stories do not deal necessarily with poor people; in several of the poems, the people obviously are living in financial comfort, and in others, the action has nothing to do with economic wellbeing. The stories also are not the exclusive property of the un-educated; several deal quite clearly with persons of considerable education and culture.

What, then, ties these stories together? The most important tie is simply the fact that they tell stories that give some satisfaction to the reader and at the same time communicate a sense of place. All the stories are based on ideas I have gathered from reading, conversation, or memory. Where I have used material based on memory, I have checked the material with at least one other person. In other words, even though I have taken the liberty of treating the material imagi-natively, the basic outlines of the stories are more than just the products of my own imagination.

All the stories are based on events that were reported to have taken place in Arkansas. However, many stories are quite similar to some found in other parts of the country and indeed in other countries. Therefore, I hope that Arkansans as well as others can enjoy reading stories that remind them of something that may have been told in their parts of the country, too.

It must be remembered that although much of the material is based on reading, the poems are being presented as a work of imagination.

I hope the poems will be interesting, entertaining, and in some cases, amusing.

Ruth Couch
Beebe, Arkansas
January 1991

The Indians at Evergreen

In the early part of this century, Mrs. Martha Wright recalls, a band of
Indians sought the help of her father, a physician in Judsonia.

The roving Cherokees were grieved
    Within their little band;
Their princess-child was very ill,
    Too weak to lift a hand.

They sought the modern doctor's help
    Toward the end of day;
The doctor's daughter gave the word
    Her father was away.

She held the young one's dainty hand
    And bathed her fevered head.
She bade the Indians go to town
    For other help instead.

The Indians made their camp at dusk
    A little way from town,
Prepared a bed as best they could
    And laid their princess down.

At dawn the fragile royal girl
    Had lost the strength to live;
The ancient chant to mourn their child
    Was all that they could give.

And near the white men's last abode
    They laid their child to rest.
With tribal rite and rhythmic dance
    Her memory was blest.

For many years they came each time
    The fateful day went by
And danced for her who left their tribe
    That day in hot July.

Based on: Wright, Martha. Quoted in W. E. Orr, "Child's Grave Dates Back
to 1890s." *White County Record.* Thursday, July 14, 1977, p. 4.

Spirit Lake

Spirit Lake is in southwest Arkansas near Lewisville. This picturesque but mysterious spot is a favorite of fishermen, although some people do indeed prefer not to let darkness catch them there.

The lakeside land was lined with trees so thick
    That limbs had twined within the wood,
Except where cotton stretched in even lines
    And houses owned by farmers stood.

The lake was nameless many, many years,
    And people rowed across to meet
And visit friends and neighbors thereabout
    Or fished, or swam, or cooled their feet.

One summer eve an aging black man left
    To visit friends awhile that night;
The neighbors watched him row across and land,
    But halfway back, they lost the sight.

They dragged the lake, but never found a trace
    Of man or boat or even oar,
Made many searches; days and months went by,
    But never did they see him more.

But, some folks say, at times when darkness falls,
    His image floats across the lake,
A lamp in front with palest, shaky flame,
    And never splash nor sound of wake.

And some have even said they'd crawl a mile
    To keep from passing there at night
For fear they'd meet the tragic missing man,
    Or see his dim and trembling light.

Based on: W. K. McNeil (ed). *Ghost Stories from the American South*. Little Rock: August House, 1985.

The Butter Fight

I have heard similar stories elsewhere. The story is interesting to me primarily for the picture it gives of Arkansas family life and the independent spirit of Arkansans.

The churning was over;
  The butter was done;
The children were ready
  To stir up some fun.

They grabbed little handfuls
  And threw at the wall;
It seemed in a moment
  They'd splatter it all.

A neighbor was watching
  And hastened to tell
That things after churning
  Weren't going too well.

The mother was angry,
  But seething still more
To see such a snooper
  So soon at her door.

"Now I didn't ask you
  To come over here;
I don't manage your folks;
  I don't interfere.

"And you ain't the one
  Got a reason to mutter,
'Cause them is my kids,
  And that is my butter!"

Based on: McDonough, Nancy. *Garden Sass: A Collection of Arkansas Folkways*. New York: Coward, McCann and Geoghegan, 1975.

Petit Jean

Petit Jean Mountain, near Morrilton, is the site of beautiful, rustic Mather Lodge, a popular retreat for vacationers. From the summit, one can enjoy the panoramic view and visit the site which some believe is the grave of Petit Jean, a lovely French girl who disguised herself as a boy in order to follow her lover.

The sun is bright, the weather fine
    On Petit Jean today;
And countless people climb the hill
    But few the higher way.

That path is rough and hard to keep,
    And bushes grow around,
And so, not many leave the road
    And climb the rocky ground.

But some will find the monument
    To faithful Petit Jean;
A picket fence around a grave
    Concealed when trees are green.

Long years ago in classic France
    The lovely Adrienne
Was broken-hearted, left alone
    By him, her treasured one.

He sought adventure, left to roam
    America's broad land,
Refused to let her share his goal
    In spite of all she'd planned.

Their hostile parents blessed the day
    He had in mind to leave;
They hardly guessed how deep her love
    Nor knew how much she'd grieve.

She wept for days, then formed a scheme
    To sail as cabin boy;
And so while plotting drastic plans,
    She treasured boundless joy.

She cast her satin gowns aside
    And donned the sailors' blue,
Her tumbling curls she clipped away,
    Put off her jewels, too.

And so they sailed; she found her love,
    And, often by his side,
She served, unrecognized by him,
    And knew a secret pride.

The men admired their Petit Jean;
    She kept the crew in cheer.
But never once her lover knew
    The one he once held dear.

The months went by; the sea trip done,
    The group explored the land;
They saw the south; and she, still strong,
    Remained within their band.

At last they came to Arkansas
    And climbed the steep terrain
And gasped to see, from high above,
    The green and growing plain.

The land was good, the group content,
    But summer passed, and fall,
And then the men began to tire
    And heard their homeland call.

And Adrienne at last was sad,
    And shivering and ill;
And strangely, too, her lover pined
    And lost his strength and will.

"The time has come; I'm going home,"
    He said to her one day;
"I'll find my lovely girl in France
    And wed her if I may."

Now gravely ill, she lost her hope
    And clung to him and cried
And told him how she left her home
    In hopes to be his bride.

"Oh, what is this I've done to you,
    To make you risk your life
And live as servant Petit Jean
    And not my honored wife?"

He buried her atop the mount
    And knew his life was done;
Before the time of budding leaves
    He joined his precious one.

The years have come; the years have gone,
    The rain and winter snow;
The grave of Petit Jean keeps watch
    On golden land below,

A shrine to loyalty and hope,
    To love that meets the test.
Step lightly, stranger, trouble not
    Our Petit Jean at rest.

Based on: Eno, Clara B. "Legends of Arkansas." *The Arkansas Historical Quarterly* (March 1943), 34–35, and Knoop, Faith Yingling, and James R. Grant. *Arkansas: Yesterday and Today*. Chicago: J. B. Lippincott Co.,1935, pp. 130–131.

The Legend of War Eagle

Each autumn the War Eagle Fair in northwest Arkansas attracts
thousands of artists and viewers. Legend tells us that the beauti-
ful river on whose banks the fair is held was the scene of a tragic
love story.

Now the War Eagle River is gentle today;
    The stones at the bottom are clean.
The artists and crafters are camped on the hillside
    As far as their tents can be seen.

The mist from the banks of the river is rising;
    There's chill in the thick autumn air,
And eagerly folk from afar have come seeking
    The fabulous War Eagle Fair.

By hundreds and thousands they visit the scene
    Entranced by the river's spell,
Yet only a few ever heard of the story
    This murmuring river could tell:

A story that's laden with sorrow and longing,
    A story of love and of woe,
Of War Eagle, son of a Cherokee chieftain,
    Who haunted these banks long ago.

Enamored he was of a beautiful maiden,
    A princess, the young Se-quah-de,
And she on her part was in love with him also
    And vowed that his bride she would be.

They planned a traditional wedding when summer
    Brought corn to a deep shade of green.
Alas for the maiden -- alas for the brave one --
    That wedding would never be seen.

For there in the Indian homeland a trapper,
    Pretending to come as a friend,
In treachery left with the beautiful maiden
    And brought all their plans to an end.

Forbidden to leave the confines of his homeland,
    He nonetheless raised him a band
Of loyal supporting companions to seek her
    Afar in a wilderness land.

At last they arrived at an Arkansas village
    And stopped to inquire for the maid.
At once the white villagers mustered a posse;
    The red men had made them afraid.

Evading the violent posse behind them,
    The braves lost the sight of their trail.
In terror they camped in the dark Boston Mountains
    And knew they were destined to fail.

To War Eagle all of them fervently pleaded
    And begged that he call off the quest;
The mountains, the forests so dense and uncharted,
    Had posed an impossible test.

At last, in an ambush he murdered a white man,
    And all of his friends fell away.
The white men were hot on his trail like a predator;
    Still, he determined to stay.

He staggered one night to the smoke of a campfire
    And crouched in the bushes to spy.
He watched as his lover was quietly cooking
    A meal for her captor nearby.

Though weakened from hunger, from grief and suspense,
    He sprang like a beast after prey --
A mistake, for the campsite was heavily guarded,
    And guns took his spirit away.

Se-quah-de, in desperate grief for her lover,
    Was granted her tearful request:
To hold ceremonial mourning for him,
    For the one she had always loved best.

But her life-force was broken, her days at an end;
    Her grieving consumed her away,
And there on the banks of the War Eagle River
    They slumber in union today,

Untroubled by footsteps of thousands of seekers
    Who visit these hills in their glory
And gasp at the radiant beauty of autumn
    Made nobler by War Eagle's story.

Based on: Steele, Phillip W. *Ozark Tales and Superstitions*. Gretna, Louisiana: Pelican Publishing Company, Inc., 1983.

War Eagle —The Meeting

(For Melinda and Jack, who met at the Fair)

Again the age-old crafts are plied;
Again the artists work with pride.

The river, scene of ancient woe,
Sees other ages come and go.

Again it works its ancient spell,
And love and romance come to dwell.

No Indian maid, this dark-eyed child,
Her features sweet, her manner mild,

Is learning arts of other days,
Preserving settlers' works and ways.

To teens she grows, and year by year,
She works her craft with others here.

And here one day, in silent joy,
She met a bright-eyed, smiling boy.

And year by year their friendship grew
And turned to love both deep and true.

Unlike the tale of Indian strife,
These two in time were man and wife.

And so where love was once denied,
They live and flourish, side by side.

Based on: Adams, Melinda. "Met Mate at War Eagle," *The War Eagle Fair Book*. Branson, Missouri: The Ozarks *Mountaineer*, 1984.

White Oak Silver Mine

In the growing village of Beebe around 1890, there were reports of a silver mine somewhere in the country nearby. The rumors were forgotten, but years later experts think the mine may really have existed.

Old Tom was a miner, but no one could say
The direction he took when he left every day.

The townspeople knew him, but no one but Matt
Would stop in the sidewalk a minute to chat.

He begged, "Take me out there; I swear not to tell."
But Tom wouldn't take him; he knew very well.

"Oh, no," Tom would tell him, "you're only a kid.
You'd blab it through Beebe, the first thing you did."

At last came a time when he needed the boy,
And so he devised an ingenious ploy.

He cornered the child and then dragged him aside
(The alley was empty, a good place to hide)

"Hey, young 'un," he said in his quavery voice,
"I need you to help me; I ain't got a choice."

They climbed in the buckboard and rattled away
At noontide that blistering late-summer day.

"Now, boy, don't you cross me; I'll give you five Troy.
But sing to your folks, and they're missing a boy."

Tom knotted a blindfold across Matthew's face
To keep him from finding a path to retrace,

And Matt had a vision that chilled to the bone
Of drifter John Markley, who vanished alone

After bragging of silver he stole from the mine
And strutting in clothing entirely too fine.

At last they arrived at a big gaping hole.
The blindfold was loosened, yet Tom kept control.

They worked for an hour to shore up the vein,
And Matt was engraving the scene in his brain.

Yet true to his word, he was silent as death.
About his adventure he spoke not a breath.

The leaves went to scarlet; the holidays neared,
And Tom, with no warning, one day disappeared.

And later, much later, young Matthew would tell
The secret he knew but had guarded so well.

And now as the years and the decades go by
The old ones at Beebe remember and sigh

And wonder if deep in the leaf-covered ground
The men and the silver will someday be found.

Based on: Pierron, Gary. "Silver in Them Hills." *Beebe Banner*. Sunday, Dec. 21, 1986, 12A, 13A.

The Lazy Man

Stories of hard work are part of the mythology of the days when the independent farm family could still eke out a living. So it is only natural that the lazy person should be an object of scorn. This story, which was told by my parents, Ben and Zettie Sanders Couch of Magnolia, was set in south Arkansas in the pre-Depression days. I have taken poetic liberty with the man's name and with the method he chose to end his life.

That Elmer Crook was lazy
    The neighbors all agreed.
He never hoed the garden
    Or stooped to pull a weed.

His wife and all his children
    Made out the best they could.
They plowed the fields and toted
    The water and the wood.

At last old El decided
    To end this earthly life:
It hurt him so to watch her,
    His overburdened wife.

His boys hitched up the wagon
    And helped their father round;
They headed for the river
    Where Elmer would be drowned.

The neighbors saw them passing
    And begged them not to go.
"We'll give him some potatoes
    Since his don't ever grow."

"But air they dug?," he asked them.
    "Well, silly, no!" they said.
"Then drive on, boys," he ordered;
    "I'd just as soon be dead!"

A similar story is told by Mrs. Alberta Richie of the Sunny Gap community east of Conway. In her story the lazy man and his wife had eaten

dinner with Mrs. Richie's parents, Dr. and Mrs. George Harrod, Sr., who had made the offer of the extra potatoes. The man's answer was the same: "Air they dug?" But his response to the answer was less dramatic; he merely refused the offer and went home.

The Cat-Bag Legend

One warm day in summer a lady was sad;
The kitty was sick, and he looked pretty bad.

At last the poor kitty could take it no more
And calmly expired on the living room floor.

"Now what can I do here?" the lady did cry,
"With you to get rid of, and groceries to buy?

"I guess I will take you to Garbage Dump Hill;
I sure hate to do it, but reckon I will."

And now she has bagged him and gone to the car
And headed for Dump Hill, a distance quite far;

And she in a dither, with bread to be bought,
Stops in at the food mart; she's certain she ought.

"Now Kitty, you lie here," she says to the sack.
"I'll grab a few items and hurry right back."

Along comes a klepto in search of a thrill,
And ogles the package, as pilferers will.

"I'll bet there's a steak for my company meal.
I guess I'll just take it -- I wouldn't say *steal*.

I know the policeman's out walking his beat,
But I can outstep him, for something to eat."

The lady was baffled, beyond any doubt,
On finding that Kitty was nowhere about,

But she not so much as the hungry young sinner
When ready to charcoal the Sunday night dinner!

> This story was circulated in the central Arkansas area, and I heard it told as
> truth in at least three different versions during the early 1970s. Usually both
> characters are women, but I have written the poem in such a way that the
> unlucky thief could be a man or a woman.

19

The Crossett Light

A similar light has also been noted at Gurdon, some miles nearer to the center of the state. In this story a railroad worker had also been killed, but the details are not as specific. There is another very famous light at Joplin, Missouri.

The Crossett woods extend for miles.
　　The branches intertwine
Across the roads like arbor roofs
　　Of dark and dismal pine.

At night the woods are dense and close
　　Along the aging rails.
The train, as always, rattles by;
　　Its mournful whistle wails.

The forest shudders, then grows still.
　　The rumble fades away;
And then there comes an eerie sight --
　　Or so the townsfolk say.

For, standing there where roadways cross
　　Some dark and dreary night,
The lonely walker peers ahead
　　And sees a waving light.

Not five feet high, the light is small
　　But bright and very clear;
It shines for moments, never more,
　　And then will disappear.

Long years ago, the homefolks say,
　　A railroad worker died,
And here his wife with weary steps
　　For years has walked and cried.

She haunts the site where long ago
　　They found her husband dead,
His body limp across the tracks,
　　But never found his head.

And so the light will move away
    And then appear again.
Determined still, she totters on
    In moonlight or in rain.

They never see her, those who walk
    These lonely rails at night.
Yet years from now they still will come
    To see the Crossett light.

Based on: Buckner, John Wordy. *Wilderness Lady*. Little Rock: Rose Publishing Company, 1979.

The Crossett Light Revisited

> Old-timers say that the mysterious light often seen at night on the railroad near Crossett is a very favorable omen for lovers. I have taken one small liberty here: I don't think the grandfather made the recommendation. I think he just reported the results.

Sweet Gertie loved her Melvin:
    She loved him very well;
She'd meet him after supper
    And visit for a spell.

Now Melvin wanted Gertie
    To be his loving bride,
But every time he hinted
    She shook her head and sighed.

He wondered and he worried
    About his luckless plight
Till Grandpa recommended
    They see the Crossett light.

They stumbled through the darkness;
    They found the narrow trail;
They saw the lantern shining
    A long way down the rail.

The night was dark and spooky;
    Poor Gertie was a wreck!
She screamed with all her power
    And grabbed her Melvin's neck.

Not more than two weeks later
    The happy neighbors heard
That Mel had asked, and Gertie
    Had given him her word.

Based on: Buckner, John Wordy. *Wilderness Lady*. Little Rock: Rose Publishing Company, 1979.

The Ha'nt Tree

Great-Grandpa hated driving late
    And passing by the tree
Where years ago his brothers died
    Before his folk were free.

The Ha'nt Tree loomed so dark and tall,
    It scared both black and white;
He feared the tree at any time
    But most of all at night.

He heard the groans of dying slaves
    Who'd crossed their master's will;
He heard a shuffling step disturb
    The night so dark and still.

He whipped his horses, tried to flee
    This place of living dead.
He turned and looked -- behind him sat
    A man without a head.

Too scared to stop, too stiff to speak,
    He beat the horses on;
A few miles later, looked around --
    His ghostly guest was gone.

And ever after, all his life
    Until his dying day,
He never passed the tree again,
    But drove the longer way.

Based on: Patterson, Ruth Polk. *The Seed of Sally Good'n*. Lexington, Kentucky: The University Press of Kentucky, 1985.

The Smallden Well

Patterson explains that some stories about ghosts and "haints" were perpetuated to keep children away from old wells, vacant houses, or other potentially dangerous places. I have taken the liberty to write about what might have happened to a child who tried to ignore such a warning.

The darkness was falling; the child was alone.
The figure addressed him in quavering tone.

"Oh, what are you doing, you bright-eyed young man,
And why are you lagging as late as you can?"

"Your house is so big, and your roses so pink,
The nicest I ever have looked at, I think."

"And why are you stopping so near to my gate?
It's dark in the yard, and you're out mighty late."

"Your myrtles are pretty, so fluffy and red;
I wish I could pick some," the little boy said.

"It's dangerous here on the Smalldens' farm;
Go home to your mother; you might come to harm.

Don't turn at my gate and don't step on my trail,"
She yelled at the child in a menacing wail.

Her face was all withered, her lanky hair white,
Her stooping old body a pitiful sight.

He watched as she floated from gatepost to well,
But what happened then, he could never retell.

He noticed her next on the well-casing rim,
And then she was gone -- or the light had grown dim.

He scurried away, taking hardly a breath,
In terror of torture or possibly death.

And never again was his mother afraid
He would idle there later than afternoon shade.

Based on: Patterson, Ruth Polk. *The Seed of Sally Good'n*. Lexington, Kentucky: The University Press of Kentucky, 1985.

Belle Starr's Race

Belle Starr is known mainly as an outlaw who lived in Fort Smith in
the late 19th century. What is not quite so well known is that she
was a woman of cultured tastes in clothing, music, art, and gracious
living. She was fiercely loyal to her loved ones and was interested
in the cause of the poor and the oppressed. Her values, however,
violated society's codes at many points. Thus she may truly be
called a 19th-century anti-heroine.

Belle Starr was quite a lady,
    The old ones used to say;
She helped the poor and needy
    And caused the rich to pay.

She loved good food and music,
    But horses best of all.
She bought a Kansas sorrel
    To grace her private stall.

She rode him back so proudly,
    But near her dwelling place
She found a worthy rival
    And challenged him to race.

The horse, a mighty stallion,
    Was huge and sleek and black.
John Hargrove, wealthy horseman,
    Was master of the track.

"I'll bet you, Mr. Hargrove,"
    She dared the startled man,
"If your horse wins, five hundred;
    I don't believe he can."

She hired an Indian jockey
    And told him what to do:
Let Hargrove's horse be winner,
    At least a length or two.

She lost, and paid the money,
  And said his horse was best.
But "just for luck" she dared him
  To set another test.

She made the stakes five thousand,
  And quickly he agreed,
So sure his horse was better
  And would, of course, succeed.

The people came to see it;
  They came from miles around.
They stood on stumps and boxes
  To see the hoofbeats pound.

She told the Indian jockey
  To let her horse run free.
The stallion lagged behind him
  And Belle was full of glee.

But never had John Hargrove
  In country or in town
Let man or beast or woman
  So firmly put him down.

And Belle was riding homeward,
  Her money in her sack,
As he was yelling curses
  At her departing back.

Based on: Steele, Phillip W.. *Ozark Tales and Superstitions*. Gretna, Louisiana: Pelican Publishing Company, Inc., 1983.

A Highway Shrine

(Highway 67, north of Judsonia)

A hundred years have come and gone;
    A hundred seasons' cycles turned,
A hundred summers, rich with bloom;
    A hundred autumn fires have burned.

A sleepy highway town has grown;
    The noise of commerce surges by,
And yet the single stone remains,
    Its outline stark against the sky.

A stately tree, a tiny yard
    The little grave enclosed, alone
Stand mutely by, a silent shrine
    To one whose name cannot be known.

A tiny girl was laid to rest,
    Her kin too poor for churchyard fees
Her sleeping-place the farmyard lot,
    Her marker, just the shady trees.

The years went by; the memory lived,
    And yellow flowers cheered her space
Each spring; in fall the leaves were raked
    And neighbors cleared the solemn place.

And then the big new road was built.
    The crews moved in; the fields were planed,
The old familiar landmarks razed,
    But still the grave and tree remained.

A decade passed, and Judson town
    In tribute bought a marble stone.
At last the tiny girl belonged --
    The town had made the child their own.

And so the years shall cycle on,
    And tourists driving by can see
How much that tiny life has meant
    And just how kind a town can be.

Based on: Orr, W.E. "Child's Grave Dates Back to 1890's." *White County Record*. Thursday, July 14, 1977, 4.

Robin Hood of Civil War Arkansas

Alone as a widow at age thirty-three
The sad Frances Gordon had nowhere to flee.

The county was wretched with hardship and war
A deadly invasion had spread from afar.

Her children were hungry; her livestock was gone,
And only through courage she dared to go on.

One day at her doorstep a rider appeared
In search of some handouts, the family feared.

They let him come in, and they gave him a plate;
And also his brother and partners all ate.

The rider then noticed the tears on her face
And pitied her plight in this war-weakened place.

He thanked her profusely and galloped away,
For he and his men were reluctant to stay;

And clearing the table that evening she found
That money was left under plates all around.

Delighted, she counted; the total was high;
Now she and her children could surely get by.

The donors had left without giving their names:
These merry companions -- and wild Jesse James!

Based on: Gray, Betty L. Gordon. "Mother of Eight Receives Help from Jesse James." *The (Searcy) Daily Citizen*. Sesquicentennial Edition. November 3, 1986, p. 10.

Hardin's Inn

> (Near Holland, in Faulkner County)

The year was eighteen fifty-five
  (And humans yet enslaved).
The forests stretched for miles on end,
  And not a road was paved.

The farmers drove their hogs and cows
  In herds to Cadron dock
Where barges left with heavy loads
  To distant Little Rock.

The Clinton road was used by all
  Whose travels crossed the state.
Thus many stopped at Hardin's Inn
  And slept, and drank, and ate.

His slaves and he had built the inn
  Of logs; and twenty guests
Could pen their cows and stash their gold
  And take their evening rest.

At times a guest would enter in
  And never more be seen
(The times were hard, the travel rough,
  The boarders sometimes mean).

As time went by, the inn did well;
  Its host grew very rich,
But rumors flew, and people feared
  The back-yard drainage ditch.

The year was nineteen fifty-five,
  And Ed was riding home.
The hill where Hardin's Inn had stood
  Was not a place to roam.

The bottom-land was dense with growth;
    The moon was very pale;
He thought he heard, beyond the ditch,
    A muffled, trembling wail.

He spurred his horse a little more
    Recalling tales of old
Of limping figures, lights, and moans
    That other folk had told.

Before his horse could gain its speed
    The headless man appeared,
His dog beside him, running fast --
    The horror Ed had feared.

The figure mounted, took the reins,
    And Ed jumped off and ran.
He ran so hard he left the horse
    And lost the headless man.

At home when asked about the ghost
    And how he had the speed
To win the race and reach his barn
    Before the trusty steed,

He caught his breath and shook his head
    But didn't want to talk --
Nor go to see, another night,
    The headless horseman walk!

Based on: Treadway, Tyler. "Tales of 19th Century. . . Still Told Around Hardin Hill." *Log Cabin Weekender* (Conway), Sunday, Oct. 28, 1984, p. 3.

The Spirit Dog

Two boys had been to "meeting,"
    And riding home that night
They strayed behind the wagon --
    The moon was big and bright.

They walked beside the creekbank.
    The others rode ahead.
The boys explored the bottoms
    A little while instead.

They spied a little creature,
    A silent, white-haired dog,
Who leaped and bounded forward,
    Its feet concealed in fog.

They watched the creature coming,
    And one picked up a stone;
The tiny dog ignored it --
    With not a whine or moan.

The rock had gone beyond him
    And landed on the ground.
He floated on toward them
    With not the slightest sound.

One boy took aim to kick it --
    His foot hit empty air.
The boys then fled in terror
    And left it floating there.

"We're sure to get a whipping
    'Cause Gramps will say we lied.
We never could convince him,
    No matter how we tried."

Their grandpa asked them later,
    At home, and short of breath
"Well, fellows, what's the matter?
    You look as pale as death."

"Now Granpa, we won't tell you
　　Unless you give your word
You won't go out and whip us
　　As soon as you have heard.

We know it sounds like lying,
　　But yet it's true, we swear."
They told about the ghost dog
　　That gave them such a scare.

"Well, boys, I've never told it
　　To any living souls,
But I have seen the ghost-dog
　　On many moonlight strolls.

When riding by the creekbank
　　Returning from a trip
I've often seen the creature
　　And chased it it with my whip.

The dog would try to chase me --
　　At times get very near --
A hundred yards or better
　　And then would disappear.

I never told it, fellows,
　　For people might have said
That Gramp was superstitious
　　Or touched within the head!"

Based on: Goolsby, Edwin L. "Historically Speaking." *The Sheridan Head-light*, Wednesday, March 14, 1984.

39

The Land Avenges

In the twenties and thirties the town of El Dorado in south Arkansas grew
rapidly because of the discovery of oil. The informant who shared this story
indicated that the man probably had a heart attack because of the state of
tension in which his remorse had caused him to live.

He never wanted oil wells;
    He loved his peaceful farm.
He feared machines and drilling
    Would bring him only harm.

The drillers tried persuasion,
    But still he wouldn't yield.
At night they turned to mayhem
    And shot him in the field.

They didn't drill that summer;
    They didn't drill that fall;
The claim was still unsettled;
    They couldn't drill at all.

The seasons hastened swiftly;
    The land was left alone.
A city grew from oil camps
    And came into its own.

At last the son permitted
    A crew to come and drill.
A silent older roughneck
    Was working with them still.

The roughneck dreaded working
    This once-contested land.
He lived in constant terror,
    A tremor in his hand.

And then one night while doing
    Their normal night routine
The workers heard a rumble:
    The oil would soon be seen.

The old man stood there stricken
    As if beneath a spell
While others worked at capping
    The quickly gushing well.

They tried, but couldn't cap it;
    The flow came out the top.
The roughneck screamed, "It's blood, it's blood!"
    And then they saw him drop.

The gleaming liquid covered
    His frame from head to toe. . . .
Before the men had finished,
    The well had ceased to flow.

They bore away his body
    And worked that field no more:
The earth itself had evened
    The long-unsettled score.

Based on: McNeil, W. K. (ed.) *Ghost Stories from the American South*. Little Rock: August House, 1985.

The Last Ride Home

Years ago, the traveler from the southern part of the state would have to
brake almost to a complete stop for a sharp, very dangerous curve a few
miles out of Little Rock. I have heard several versions of this story. Al-
though I have taken some points from McNeil, much of this version is as it
was told to me about twenty years ago when I drove to Little Rock from
Magnolia and expressed my concern about the dangerously sharp curve in
the old road a few miles south of the city.

The driver, tired from many miles
    Of narrow, twisting, tree-lined road,
Became alert at traffic signs,
    Applied his brake, and smoothly slowed

In time to make the sharpest curve.
    The road was black and wet and slick.
Alone, he shuddered, feeling chilled.
    The woods beyond were dark and thick.

A human figure, hair in ruin,
    Its garment trailing, long and white,
Raised up a slender hand and waved
    Within the narrow band of light.

He stared in disbelief at first,
    But something somehow caught his eye --
Her rain-soaked dress, her pale-blue coat --
    And wouldn't let him pass her by.

She pled with him to take her home.
    Her date had left the prom, she said,
And she was all alone to walk
    The dreary miles that lay ahead.

Arriving home, she seemed afraid
    And asked if he perhaps would go
And meet her mother at the door,
    The midnight darkness scared her so.

The light was on, but pale and blue;
    The care-worn mother soon replied:
"My daughter can't be here with you;
    Ten years ago this night she died!"

"That can't be true! She's in the car.
    Just come along yourself and see!
Her date had left her; she was scared
    And glad to get a ride with me!"

The mother staggered to the car;
    The driver opened wide the door:
The girl was gone, and nothing there
    But drops of water on the floor.

"My daughter left ten years ago!
    A late-night wreck in fog and rain
Has taken all our joy away,
    And nights like this renew the pain."

She saw the man was not convinced
    And had him drive her miles away
To where a tombstone marked the spot
    In which her lovely daughter lay.

The headlights brought the grave in sight.
    A gasp of terror closed his throat,
For there across the marble slab
    Was draped the rain-drenched pale-blue coat!

Based on: McNeil, W. K. (ed.). *Ghost Stories from the American South*. Little Rock: August House, 1985.

The Late-Night Shortcut

Although I have followed Mr. Wisdom's story here, I have also encountered variations of it in southern Arkansas. The story is usually told as an example of what can be done with proper motivation.

At ten Dave headed homeward
    -- His working day just done --
Three miles by graveled roadway,
    By shortcut, only one.

The road was long and tiring.
    The shortcut, filled with dread,
Would take him through the graveyard
    Among the silent dead.

His aching legs decided
    To take the shorter way.
He knew the path to follow
    And thought he wouldn't stray.

The ironwork gate was opened --
    The hinges creaked aloud.
The treelimbs shuddered darkly --
    The moon behind a cloud.

He touched a dewy tombstone
    As tall as he, or more,
That honored one departed
    A hundred years before.

The starlight glimmered palely
    On lamb-adorned small tombs;
His nostrils caught the fragrance
    Of old and withered blooms.

He tiptoed through the section
    Where kin and loved ones lay;
He heard the long-lost voices
    From childhood's early day.

At last, his pulses beating,
    He spied the distant fence --
The moon a ghostly halo,
    The clouds still dark and dense.

The light at this point failed him.
    His feet began to slide.
He stumbled, lost his balance,
    And lurched from side to side.

He tumbled headlong downward
    Within a new-dug grave.
He struggled, gained his balance,
    And then began to rave.

He clawed the muddy dirtwall;
    He jumped with all his might.
He tried to get a toehold;
    He yelled with rabid fright.

At last he fell exhausted
    And cowered in the mud.
His heart was wildly racing
    And panic chilled his blood.

A voice beside him whispered,
    "I'm trapped here too, you see.
You can't get out till morning!
    Just sit, and talk to me!"

Now Dave had no intention
    To chat beneath the ground,
And so he gained his freedom
    In one heroic bound!

Based on: Wisdom, Walter. "This and That." *The Beebe News*, January 22,
1987, p. 7.

Aunt Mollie's Warning

The mythical hoop snake is supposed to form a wheel by grabbing his tail between his jaws. In this position he is supposed to roll like a wagon wheel at incredible speed. He grabs his victim and whips him unmercifully. The only way to escape is to jump through his circle.

"Beware the dreaded hoop snake;
    He's sneakin' in the grass;
No matter how you tiptoe,
    He hears you when you pass.

The rattlesnake is awful;
    The moccasin is mean;
But folks, I swear, the hoop snake's
    The worst I ever seen!

He's mighty big and ugly
    A-huntin' him a meal;
He makes a great big circle
    And travels like a wheel.

No way can you outrun him,
    No matter how you try.
He'll wrap his tail around you
    And beat you till you die!

He'll chase you through the cornfield,
    The yard and pasture too.
There's just one way to lose him,
    And this is what you do.

You let him roll beside you
    And jump right through the loop
The way a young-un playin'
    Would try to jump a hoop.

That way, you get him flustered.
    He'll fall and slink away.
You're safe from dreaded hoop snakes
    At least another day.

But let me tell you, children,
    That's mighty hard to do.
You'd better just avoid him
    Before he chases you.

What's that? You don't believe me?
    You think I'm tellin' lies?
Oh, no! I seen a dozen
    Before my very eyes!"

This story was told to me in south Arkansas by a young black woman
about 1955.

The Prisoner from Little Rock

> The first six stanzas of this poem are composed in the form of a dialogue,
> with the speakers alternating. The first speaker is the officer, and the second
> is the prisoner. In the seventh stanza, the storyteller picks up the narration.
> Dialogues are quite common in ballads.

> We'll go to the courthouse and there you'll be tried
> And pay with your life, because Sarah has died.

I'm guiltless of Sarah, the love of my life,
The one I had wanted to take as my wife.

> We found you, you know, in the mossy old well
> And though you are silent, the murder will tell.

I weep for dear Sarah; my heart is in pain
While I'm chained at your side in the back of this train.

> I shouldn't have loosed you to let you relax;
> You might have been killed when you jumped to the tracks.

I wish I had fallen and died at the time,
Since Sarah is gone, and I'm charged with the crime.

They took him to Perryville, tried him as planned,
Decreed that he die at the hangingman's hand.

Protesting his innocence, yet without hope,
At last he was dead by the strength of the rope.

The years flew apace and the customs were changed;
The rope was laid up, and new justice arranged.

At last in the county an old man was ill,
The father of him who so long had been still.

He called for the marshal to come to his bed,
And making confession, he haltingly said:

My son that was hanged was an innocent boy --
I never could share him, my pride and my joy,

With any young woman, and least of all her --
I killed her in hopes we could live as we were!"

Mr. Wisdom states that this young man was the last person to be hanged legally in Arkansas. The time was about 1914.

Based on: Wisdom, Walter. *90 Years of Short Stories*. Privately printed.

The Hook

The Bluff was beautiful that spring:
    The songs of whippoorwills nearby --
The moon above -- the fluffy clouds --
    The velvety expanse of sky.

The car was stopped, and not a word
    Disturbed the peace of mellow air.
Two students sat: a handsome boy,
    A girl with silky raven hair.

A thrill -- or dread -- within her heart
    Had made her slightly ill at ease,
And then a newscast coming on
    Had caused her trembling heart to freeze.

"A convict, just escaped from jail,
    Is missing somewhere near the bluff;
One hand is gone; he wears a hook;
    His skin is scarred and very rough."

"Oh, please, let's go," she begged the boy.
    "I hate it being here tonight!"
"Oh, hush! He's miles away, I'm sure,
    And hiding somewhere out of sight."

A wind came up; the treelimbs swayed
    Against the car and scratched the side.
Her fears intensified, they left;
    And she, now panicked, sobbed and cried.

Arriving back on campus then
    He walked around to get her door
And stared like one who walks asleep
    And gasped in shock, but said no more.

The girl dashed out to see the cause
    And took one dreadful, frenzied look --
There, clinging to the right-hand door,
    Was clenched the awful convict's hook,

And some folks say that when he turned
    And saw her standing in the light,
The lovely hair so long and black
    Had turned to alabaster white!

    I first heard this story at Southern Arkansas University during the 1950s. Since it is very common (Brunvand, 337), I have taken the liberty of setting it in Arkadelphia, where the river bluff is a legend in itself.

The Valley of Vapors

The Kanewagos were an Indian tribe that lived near what is now Hot
Springs. They were a very proud people until illness decimated their tribe.

"Oh, Wise Man, Wise Man, tell us now,
    What evil have we done
That brings the plague on young and old
    To strike us one by one?"

Oh, Kanewagos, heed my words
    Which often you ignored;
You praised yourselves above the One
    Your fathers once adored.

You ruled thee valleys far and wide,
    Controlled both man and beast,
Forgot the Spirit, known of old,
    Who used to rule your feast.

"We grow so weak, we cannot hunt
    Nor keep the foes away.
Oh, tell us, Wise Man, what to do,
    And how we ought to pray."

Oh, Kanewagos, call the tribe
    And hold a solemn rite
And praise the Spirit's holy name
    And recognize His might.

"Our hearts have been forgiven now,
    But still with fevered brows
We seek the gentle streams and springs
    Beneath the shady boughs.

But Wise Man, we are cursed again!
    The water steams with heat.
We fear the Spirit boils with wrath
    Beneath our weary feet."

Oh, Kanewagos, you are blest.
    The Spirit loves you well.
He sends his healing waters here
    And bids you safely dwell.

"Oh, Wise Man, truly we will pledge
    To honor Him above
Who gave His healing springs to flow
    In mercy, peace, and love;

And 'Breath of Healing' we will name
    This valley where we live
To praise the Spirit, great and strong,
    And willing to forgive."

Based on: Fountain, Sarah. *Authentic Voices: Arkansas Culture, 1541–1860.* Conway: University of Central Arkansas Press, 1986.

The Shopping-Mall Specter

Her shopping done, the high-school girl
    Prepared to hurry home.
The time was late, her chores undone;
    She hadn't time to roam.

She reached her car, but strange to see
    She had an aged guest;
A dark-clad, hunch-backed woman sat
    As if to take a rest.

She looked bedraggled, tired and poor,
    Too frail to dread or fear;
And yet her brow was strangely smooth;
    Her eyes were bright and clear.

"Oh, please, in Heaven's name," she gasped,
    "A little help, I pray!
I'm sick -- I couldn't find my car --
    It's such a sultry day."

The girl drew back, a little scared,
    And made a quick reply:
"Don't go away; I'll be right back,
    And then I'll help -- or try! --"

Soon, back she dashed, police in tow,
    And seemed no little shocked
To see the mugger-dressed-as-crone
    So suddenly defrocked.

And ever after, when she stopped
    For even just a minute
She locked her car and triple-checked
    For fear of someone in it!

    This story has been told as fact two times within my hearing since 1980.
One time it was supposed to have taken place at McCain Mall at North
Little Rock.

The Hitchhiker of 1980

His suit was of navy; his hairstyle was sleek;
His manner was gracious, not craven or meek.

The elderly driver was greatly impressed
By the way that he talked, and the way that he dressed.

"I think," said the driver, " I never have seen
The country so dry, not a smidgin of green."

"How terribly true," the young passenger said
As they stared at the landscape, so barren and dead.

The rider continued, "I think it's the end,
And life will be finished quite shortly, my friend.

I think there will never again be a rain,
And the earth will conclude all its sorrow and pain."

In silence they rode in the blistering sun
And pondered the damage the summer had done.

"Well, this is my exit; I'm leaving you here,"
The driver announced when his homestead was near.

A glance to the left turned his pulses to stone,
For his rider was vanished, and he was alone.

Two versions of this story were circulated in the central Arkansas area
during the record-breaking drouth of 1980. One is supposed to have taken
place on the freeway between Little Rock and Arkadelphia.

The Black Lady Walks at Henderson State

Picturesque Henderson State University in Arkadelphia was formerly Henderson-Brown Methodist College. It is located across the street from Ouachita Baptist University. The rivalry between the two schools is legendary.

"Oh, where are you headed, you lovely young coed,
　　Your figure all hidden in somberest black?"
"I've left my good school on the solemnest mission;
　　I've crossed the ravine, and I'm not turning back."

"Oh, what are you planning this blustery evening?
　　And why have you come on this one special date?"
"I've come to the fence, with its rusty iron pickets;
　　My sorrow compels me to enter the gate."

"Oh, how can you travel this hilly dark campus,
　　Stopping for nothing, without any light?"
"I know all the trees, and the bushes and sidewalks,
　　The sundial that's timeless so late in the night."

"And why are you running so fast down the bridgewalk?
　　And how can you keep to so narrow a way?"
"I'm seeking the hall where my rival lies sleeping,
　　And oh, when I find her, at last she will pay."

"What good will it do you to win such a vengeance?
　　All ever was fair in war and in love!"
"Oh, no, he preferred me, but others prevented --
　　And that, I will swear to by all that's above!"

"Who was it that stood between you and your lover?
　　And why should they force you, unwilling, to part?"
"Oh, truly our parents, because of religion,
　　Made trouble for both of us, right from the start."

"But wasn't he bound in his heart to defend you,
    To treasure your love as he treasured his life?"
"Oh, true, but a girl of his own faith was willing,
    And I lost the strength to continue the strife.

So I stalk her each fall when the homecoming season
    Recalls the sad night I could bear it no more!
I will steal through the shadows and glide past the columns
    And find her at last if I break every door!"

> The legend of the black lady of Henderson seems to be almost as old
> as the school. In these verses I have roughly followed the 1970s
> version collected by W. K. McNeil. The version that was common in
> the fifties was that the black lady was a coed who had died in a
> tragic fire that destroyed the main building, on whose top floor the
> girls were housed. I prefer the newer version because it includes the
> strong motivating forces of love, parental opposition, and revenge,
> thus giving more credibility to the lady's impassioned search. What
> she would do if she ever found her victim was not specified.

Carry A. Nation

In the early 1900s, Carry Amelia Nation was a noted temperance worker who made her home in Eureka Springs. To help pay for her crusade against alcohol, she sold little pins in the shape of an axe. Her foes retaliated by making vinegar jars in her image, implying that she was very "sour" to go around chopping up saloons with her axe. Carry spelled her first name with a *y* and used her middle initial because her goal was to "carry a nation" toward abstinence from alcohol.

To carry a nation was always her aim,
And so she adopted this meaningful name.

Her early adulthood was riddled with strife,
Her husband a drunkard, the bane of her life.

At age fifty-five she was left on her own,
And shortly thereafter, her name was well known.

She came to Eureka promoting her cause
And flew in the face of the customs and laws.

She entered the taverns and wielded her axe,
Destroying the barstands in one or two whacks.

She opened her home to the destitute wives
Who had fled from their husbands in fear for their lives.

She told them to pay for their board and their bed
By running her kitchen, where tourists were fed.

She traveled the country and preached against drink
Without a concern for what people might think.

She was jailed; she was hated, spat on, and jeered;
And yet she grew famous respected and feared.

At last after decades her fragile frame broke;
Her travel was stopped by a life-threatening stroke.

Yet still with a voice little more than a breath
She spoke for her cause till the day of her death.

The material for this poem was gathered during a tour of her home in
Eureka Springs in August 1988.

The Roosters Crow for Christmas

In south Arkansas in the 1940s there was a folk saying that roosters crowed at midnight during the Christmas holidays. I finally discovered two other people who remembered this charming little bit of lore. The poem is in the form of a dialogue between a daughter and a mother.

"Oh, Mother, wake and listen;
    Come quick and bring a light.
I heard the old red rooster
    A-crowin' in the night."

"Go back to sleep, my daughter;
    The rooster's bound to crow;
Tonight's the birth of Jesus,
    And feathered creatures know

They crow, my dear, for Christmas
    A week or two before.
They celebrate each midnight
    An hour's time or more."

"But Mother, how do roosters
    Know this is Jesus' birth?"
-- "Go back to bed, my daughter,
    And pray for peace on earth!"

Based on: Memory. I was the daughter. This memory is confirmed by my cousin, Marie Burns of Magnolia, and my friend, Margaret Moore of Lonoke and Beebe. In England a similar idea is shown in Thomas Hardy's poem "The Oxen," in which the poet refers to the belief that farm animals kneel at midnight on Christmas eve.

Bibliography

Adams, Melinda. "Met Mate at War Eagle." *The War Eagle Fairbook*. Branson, Missouri: The Ozarks Mountaineer, 1984.

Buckner, John Wordy. *Wilderness Lady*. Little Rock: Rose Publishing Company, 1979.

Brunvand, Jan Harold. *The Study of American Folklore*. New York: W. W. Norton, 1968.

Eno, Clara B. "Legends of Arkansas." *The Arkansas Historical Quarterly II* (March 1943), 34–35.

Fountain, Sarah. (Ed.) *Authentic Voices: Arkansas Culture, 1541–1860*. Conway: University of Central Arkansas Press, 1986.

Goolsby, Elwin. "Historically Speaking." *The Sheridan (Ark.) Headlight*, Wednesday, March 14, 1984.

Gray, Betty L. Gordon. "Mother of Eight Receives Help from Jesse James." *The (Searcy) Daily Citizen*, Sesquicentennial Edition. November 3, 1986, 10.

Knoop, Faith Yingling, and James R. Grant. *Arkansas: Yesterday and Today*. Chicago: J. B. Lippincott Co., 1935.

McDonough, Nancy. *Garden Sass: A Catalog of Arkansas Folkways*. New York: Coward, McCann and Geoghegan, 1975.

McNeil, W. K. (Ed). *Ghost Stories from the American South*. Little Rock: August House, 1985.

Orr, W. E. "Child's Grave Dates Back to 1890's." *White County Record*. Thursday, July 14, 1977, 4.

Patterson, Ruth Polk. *The Seed of Sally Good'n*. Lexington, Kentucky: The University Press of Kentucky, 1985.

Pierron, Gary. "Silver in Them Hills." *Beebe Banner*. Sunday, December 21, 1986, 12A, 13A.

Steele, Phillip W. *Ozark Tales and Superstitions*. Gretna, Louisiana: Pelican Publishing Company, Inc., 1983. Rpt. 1985.

Treadway, Tyler. "Tales of 19th Century . . . Still Told Around Hardin Hill." *Log Cabin Weekender* (Conway), Sunday, October 28, 1984, 3.

Wisdom, Walter. *90 Years of Short Stories*. Copyright Walter Wisdom.

Wisdom, Walter. "This and That." *The Beebe News*, January 22, 1987, 7.

About the Illustrators

Jerry D. Poole has served as professor and chairman of the art department of the University of Central Arkansas. His doctorate in education is from the University of Arkansas. He has taught art in the public schools and has exhibited at the Dallas Museum of Fine Arts, the State Exhibition Museum at Shreveport, Arkansas State Festival of Arts at Little Rock, and numerous arts and crafts exhibitions including War Eagle Arts and Crafts Assocation. He is a member of many professional organizations, including National Art Education Association, Mid-South Watercolor Society, American Watercolor Society and the Arkansas Education Association. Special interests include silhouettes, commercial art, window display art and calligraphy. His special interest in Arkansas topics can be seen in two projects done for the University of Central Arkansas: "Contemporary Folk Painters from Eight Mid-Arkansas Counties" and "An Artist Looks at Arkansas' Highway Seven; An Exhibition of Watercolor Paintings."

Foy Lisenby has served as professor and chairman of the history department at the University of Central Arkansas. His Ph.D. is from Vanderbilt University. He has had articles published on several aspects of Arkansas history, such as "A Survey of Arkansas' Image Problem." He has presented scholarly papers at meetings of many professional associations, notably the Arkansas Historical Association, the Southwest Social Science Association, and the Popular Culture Association (Southern division). His most recent presentations include "American Women as Depicted in Magazine Cartoons, 1930-1960" and "Folklore in American Comic Art." An article on the University of Arkansas appears in the *Encyclopedia of American Culture.*